THE HEART'S
CLOCKWORK

BRIAN HINTON

THE HEART'S CLOCKWORK

with illustrations by
JULIAN BELL

ENITHARMON PRESS 1989

First published in 1989
by the Enitharmon Press
40 Rushes Road
Petersfield
Hampshire GU32 3BW

ISBN 1 870612 55 8 (paper)
ISBN 1 870612 90 6 (cloth)

The Enitharmon Press acknowledges financial
assistance from Southern Arts

Set in Monotype (hot-metal) 11-12pt Walbaum
by Gloucester Typesetting Services
and printed by
Antony Rowe Limited, Chippenham, Wiltshire

For Eileen

The Heart's Clockwork

No more slow Victorian tick-tock, now
computerised the numbers slowly turning –
the long fuse of my life is burning
digitally, time falling weighty as snow.

Better to know time as an unseen presence
like the soul, a sea we drown in everyday
squandering – like mad children at play –
the ever whirling top of present tense

which keels over at our end. So keep it spinning,
watch TV schedules and endlessly change channel;
the videotape of existence forever running out.
Each unplanned moment is a small indecision
by which we measure out our time; tooth enamel,
wrinkles, life-lines – the clocks we cannot doubt.

CONTENTS

III

ON THE STRAND

LANDLOCKED

PREVIOUS COLLECTIONS

Bitter End
Poems From An Island
The Old Changing Way
Sotonians
Breasting the Tide

ACKNOWLEDGEMENTS

Early drafts of some of these poems have appeared in the following magazines: *Alternative Poetry, Celebration, Facets of an Island, Flint, IOW County Press, Island Images, Orbis, Ore, Quay Arts Review, Scan, South,* and *Tears in the Fence.* The opening section of 'This Island Now' was broadcast on *Radio Solent.*

'*Festival*' draws on a suite of songs written for the Welfare State production *The Dennysons of Dishwater,* performed at Carisbrooke Castle in July 1987.

My thanks are due to James Sale, who first organised these poems into a coherent structure, to David Caddy, Stephen Lee and Robert Lumsden, who provided helpful comments on work in progress, and to Dave Harris, who supplied the soundtrack.

'Silence' is dedicated to the memory of Joseph McManus (1912–1986).

A STRANGE SEA

Flints

For David Orme

'The worst storm to hit southern England for over 200 years did
not prevent fans from filling Wembley Arena last night to pay
homage to veteran folk-rocker Bob Dylan. Many left disappointed.
"It was as if he was punch-drunk," one said, "he hardly seemed
to know we were there." '

Agency Report 16.10.87

I

My childhood knew no bounds – lies fostered by experience –
but only boundaries. Uphill I trudged to school. Downhill
I flew the edges of my flat earth, warping common-sense
with sherbet, stamps 'on approval', windfalls; gorging my fill
of forever, flint-eyed at the Saturday matinée. Held in camera,
such times are gone.

Violence was all; our day-glo badges winked a constellation
as we goggled at Kimo Sabbi, Davy Crockett, the Caped Pretender.
They went down blazing, but lit a mighty conflagration
in our souls – playground wars were flints struck on dry tinder:
I wore a coon-skin cap, shot the world with my Winchester
      Repeater –
such times are gone.

Crossing early to adulthood over the library floor's parquet
I was star-struck, an astronaut to *New Worlds*. Philip E. High,
Brunner's flinty heroes, Ballard's poetics, Moorcock's malarky
were my compasses; yellow as Gollancz SF, I kept a weather eye
on English disasters, triffids fanned by a *Wind from Nowhere.*
Such times are gone.

II

Years circle, vengeful Indians round a weary wagon-train.

Across the settled slopes of Southern England, that rich and resonant heartland, stutters a mad rehearsal for some monochrome catastrophe – 'The Martians have landed' – this meticulously planned and comfortable kingdom laid bare, trees flung about like Keystone cops in a cocaine-fuelled fantasy, the whole air alive and dangerous in this comic foreboding of the Great Crash – equities as savagely displaced as Shanklin pier suddenly lifted like a pickpocket's morning wallet and flung to the waves – this disarray of our cold conformity.

Such times are gone, and never were.

First light brings a tangled multiplicity, paving-stones upended by ornamental saplings, yachts beached on the road, railway lines piled high with new sleepers, analysts and weathermen too loudly protesting their innocence, supermarkets an open car boot for crazed consumers, roofs suddenly skylights, fences guarding new and strange acres, a shiny car floating in next door's swimming pool. Looters on the beach scuffle over the sea's latest harvest, coins unleashed from sunken fruit-machines like a Titanic cache of lost silver, free money spread as a banquet on the sand.

We woke to a new world, visited only in our dreams.

III

Such times are gone,
flintlock conformity unpicked by this wind from nowhere,
no fiction now, tearing like a banshee at my eyes,
timber, green-houses, trash whirled in devilish malarky;
all that I goggled at on some illicit teenage high
come to pass while I hide, scrabbling on the parquet.

Such times are gone,
as we head past a video jammed on its infinite repeater –
tree after tree after tree after tree fallen, tinder
hurled like flints by this glacier of mere air, a conflagration
devoutly to be wished on our way to see the Old Pretender
who once piped 'Blowing in the Wind', howling down
      constellations.

Such times are gone,
as he blinks shell-shocked like a victim at each cruel camera,
staring out the tempest, grinning privately. Eager eyes fill
with tears at our joint befuddlement, our weary common sense;
fists flail like branches, I punch out blindly at the downhill
of our lives. Flints can cut the heart. I mutilate experience.

Another Day

I don't feel any older until I have to reflect
on a self unseen – more ponderous around the middle,
a hairline where the tide's gone out. Less circumspect,
just as circumstantial, time's everyday riddle.

It hits me hard, as parents shrink to strangers,
friends move away, old neighbours disappear.
The pubs I grew in, their rich illicit dangers,
like unfrequented rockpools are scoured clean.

No child to inherit the old school tie, or discover
that same world. A strange sea laps my boundaries
to clear detritus of a life that's gone, covered
by salt water which corrodes me. Lost hegemonies!

Varsity Dreams

Attics are the mind's forgotten gaps;
a cache of student magazines splits open
like a simple world once up for grabs
but ungrabbable, our opportunities unspoken.

I re-read with horrified precision
manifestos which went wrong along the line,
the hopeless poses of vaunted ambition
which fail to raise a smile, given time.

All the hopeful names that never sparked;
one in twenty means anything now.
It kind of chills – like death – the heart
to see what history allowed.

Tidings

I walk the beach each evening
wait until dark has tided in,
a phantom lover exuberant as sin
I walk the beach each evening.

She leaves her clothes so neatly
on the crest of the solitary beach,
swims like a dolphin quite out of reach.
She leaves her clothes so neatly.

I sometimes think of her as if alive
swirling waves can never bury her,
in ravines far beneath the air
I sometimes think of her as if alive.

I walk the beach each evening
where daylight stretches out to dream,
in search of what has never been
I walk the beach each evening.

Push and Shove

When I catch your eyes across the dance-floor,
you're suddenly a stranger, and I'm in love
again. After all that push-and-shove,
just a touch of your hand is something more.

The more we know, the more we need to know;
seeing you bare-headed out in the rain
melts me like sunshine; I cannot regain
ever, the dent in your schoolgirl pillow,

lost scent in rooms I never now can enter.
So there you stand, proud as a naughty child
whose mother can never call her home. Smile
and come back here, my subtle heart's inventor.

Gifts

Love's alchemy transmutes not the base coin of words
but that more solid crinkle of cash – turned undeterred
from solitary pleasures to flowers, trinkets, a meal for two.
Inside bars of affection, we pace the same cage; a human zoo
watched entranced by starlings and mice, moths and spiders
who pause at our boundaries, untouched by such tame desire.

Our cat slips between two worlds, bringing us her gifts
of headless prey, curled voles sweet in death, cut adrift
from the dangerous dark – foundlings of a cold, unknowable love.
They stiffen in gross simulation of your ecstasy, paws shoved
rigid as if stretched towards me, eyes bright with painful light.
What could I bring to match her savage, fulfilled delight.

Full with pleasure, she sleeps between us, pushing us apart
masterfully. Beaten we fall back, but I feel your heart
pound just as fiercely, blind to the propinquities of love:
bodies too are endless darkness, like those laid outside, above
mere metaphysics. Rooted in the vast eternity of death
I cling to your safety, bringing simply the gift of myself.

Eating Out

Our daily bread becomes the spice of life –
gloriously variant, fry-ups and cold buffets,
barbecues, high-teas, fish suppers. The same knife
butters toast, fillets meat, pins back the plaice.

For festivals we troop to a foreign sepulchre,
knit chopsticks, fork spaghetti, unskewer kebabs;
royalty for a night until host turns entrepreneur
and shoehorns the bill, stiff with hidden tabs.

Tonight I am the jovial Raj, you my Memsahib;
here under the Taj Mahal (in sticky black and white)
sitars chuckle like the child I've never fathered;
your tikka, my tandoori chick mingle with delight.

Each plate is an event, a story to be savoured,
a history despatched. I weigh my ponderous lager
– cold as the Ganges in winter – to toast labours
of our working week. Our satisfaction is garnered

and wiped clean like each heavy, heated plate,
each shaken tablecloth in this dim-lit place
where waiters endure like untasted wedding-cake.
Life gobbles us up. An eternity of losing face.

Close Encounter

That night, the careful fabric of our love
snagged on barbed wire – I forget reasons.
What still disturbs me is the mutual treason;
tender lips bared and bright with blood.

The hurricane at last blown out, unbidden
taunts still echoing in silent air, we stared
in horror at that sudden wreckage, clung hard
together, violence resolved as indecision.

I took the air; it brought, at some crossroads
a scrabbling terror, resolved in lamplight
as a streak of low fury, massively in flight –
perhaps a badger, grubbing the moon-stained hedgerow
and put to fright, frantic claws raking asphalt,
or perhaps something other; love's sure default.

More

There is no large difference, your being here;
more washing-up, a bulging laundry basket, less room
– and yet the very room expands. You bring near
everything I once held distant. Solitude I assumed

permanent yields to the mixed pleasures of company –
someone else in the loo and my bed, a bathtime for two
where your sweet flesh so close becomes infinity –
every move is doubled, the difficult sum of you and me.

I dread losing what I never had. Exchanging clothes
and accents like billiard-balls rebounding on green baize,
we endlessly rebound on one another, put aside foes
and friends to create paradise, here and day by day.

Squalls in a teacup surge to tempest, ebb in unspoken relief
to drive us through the rags of time in our tiny barque;
you as helmsman, me as crew. Sheltered from storm and grief,
we sail the fathomless depths. I cannot imagine your lack.

Till Death

When bodies give themselves, at dawn, back to the conscious mind
– gone AWOL somewhere on coracles of darkness – we welcome
each other as if reborn, borne from night's sure kingdom
to disengage and separate at daybreak. Light, too, can blind.

Recollections of your flesh, nurtured in the day-sick brain,
transmute its rubbery fastness, its warmth. I can imagine
better than feel, and your voice is more closely certain
on the telephone than literally in my ear. Ice inflames,

fire cools our fretful being to mere ash. Life evicts
and – though it is your mind I love – it leaps forth solely
through the way it inhabits skin; to leave that lonely
at last, a perfect mask, a conjuror's discarded tricks.

Each freckle, each twist of your mind will – like my rough body – pass,
but our spirits intermingling . . . that, dear God, must somehow last.

Silence

Sitting in his chair, smoking the dried-up cigarettes
he never had time to finish, I tangle – half asleep –
with the sheer cussedness of the dead, their vexed
absence, like stubborn children playing hide-and-seek.

Nothing quite rhymes, I'm not quite ready for my bed
– the slow luxuriance of sleep – until I get it straight,
this wilful silence; so that what was never fully meant
becomes a curse, the unreached terminus of making sense.

Death is a slow choking, then sudden, unbearable light.
He came back in a dream to say 'I'm not allowed to talk
about here, but I'll tell you one thing; the food's rotten',
and then I woke back to the everyday world of lies
where we walk incomplete and shrouded beneath high walls
guarding the knowledge Eve could not digest, nor Pandora open.

THIS ISLAND, NOW

'Wrap me up in me oilskins and jumpers,
No more on the docks I'll be seen.
Tell me old shipmates,
I'm taking a trip, mates,
And I'll see you someday on Fiddlers' Green.'

Traditional

i. *Vampires*

This Island now, a place where past and future forever meet;
last year the local outlaw, revving in the street,
was bawled out by an intemperate and upright neighbour.
That night a figure rapped his door, black-favoured
with a corpse's insistence and a crow's head, hooded.
It came at him and walked through the wall, for was it
not that very night – at the dead hour – the denizen next door
burst his heart. Infinite as pebbles on the shore
is coincidence: a crow's eyes bright, sullen with violence.
How far between the dead and the living? A wilful silence.

You could crowd all the world on this island, cheek by jowl,
but what continent holds the dead. There's something foul
about the beauty here. Darkness brings drunks and spectres;
the devil in your room at Freshwater Bay. A Farringford lecture
by the local erotic exorcist – she dreamt a male nude torso
oozing ashore, initials carved on its chest; our souls
obligingly whirlpool. The police, of course, call some four
days later. 'There's something grim just come ashore . . .'
We're half in love with uneaseful death, half terror struck,
just the kind of frisson to make fortunes for video muck
in this cold time, when compassion's not only out the window
but incinerated. We wallow through the late-night horror show;
dwarves and vampires, beggar your neighbour, *Howard's Way*.

The poor are friendless, the rich so elegantly depraved.
Sin is in the deep freeze. What the Sex Pistols glamorised
is the age's *glasnost* – bitterness, envy, skating thin ice.

The kid downstairs, bemused and pony-tailed, thunders to the void
reissued CDs I treasure on vinyl – Fairport, Cream, the Floyd.
That drugged generation is grown up now, hunkering for
     sensation;
peace and love – thrown on the bonfire of zero inflation.

Frost and flame, mind you, are wise if bitter masters. They
purge the mind of weakness. On a bleak shore I watch dismayed
wave retreating onto wave, the same drab water endlessly
recycled, lapping the beach with tongues of fire, a petrol sea
I study not as 'an encounter with transcendence', but for clues
(in this garbage world we seek the wreckage for what we can use.)
Winter flaunts its bareness. Children wear black for Halloween,
whiskered and caped. Fireworks fall spent on the village green;
we face the bonfire, hot dogs burning our hands, our faces
sinister and disembodied in the glow – we could change places
with the jovial crew at an auto da fé. The summer of love burns
and we roast spuds in the ashes; crisp, plump and done to a turn.

ii. *Memorial Hall, Freshwater*

A boozy 'night out', *Talk of the Wight*. The compère, a high kicker,
seduces the gathered host to surrender, shows her knickers.
She puckers her lips to our applause, a love for herself
turns endemic. We each pay dear for this measured wealth
of gross experience. She's pirhouetted at the Windmill,
ridden the Queens, reduced herself from caviare to pigswill.
This tiny village hall, the end not of the pier but the road
– restless in the welcoming dark, the audience explodes.

Lights darken, we spread to balding ladies, pot-bellied
squires, wimps, Miss Shimbleshanks, adolescent jellies
and bemused kids, bifocal OAPs performing double-takes.
From behind the curtain, a single drum roll earthquakes.
They're on, the boys grown portly, swinging blue jeans resewn
to three-piece suits, their crackly guitars like stones thrown
through the glasshouse of our quiet lives. One Two Three
and it's Merseybeat, tight as an Elizabethan rondeau, the
call and response an echo-poem, which we echo in turn –
rock-like bass, sharp cymbals, shiny lead guitar that burns.
They swing in unison, apostles of the big beat, on the road
and in our hearts, pioneers from the wild west, a medicine show
whose potions (love, no 9) we slurp at from the fountainhead;
twitching to a rhythm which energises our minds, our beds.

Crossing the bar, we're pleasured by a foursquare clerk whose
muttonchops twitched last Sunday at Mass. He soothes
himself now with beer not holy wine, but both are rituals,
like this. The compère comes back a princess, whose initial
duty is not pleasure but community – we all bow down together
as she embarrasses to feeling. Tickly as a goose feather
she lines us up to ring handbells, blowing kisses, blessings.
The heavenly spheres crack from the heights of our imaginings.

iii. *Model Village, Godshill*

The village holds itself, complete,
like a mystery. To our endless surprise
in a model walled-off from the street
the village holds itself, complete;
diminished we tower, while at our feet
in the model of the model, a model lies –
the village, holding itself, complete.
Like a mystery too, our endless surprise.

iv. *"Fiery Creations"*

From that grey world across the water, ferried by Charon
to a magic isle, our long bedroll trek fleeing from mammon;
three pounds, ten shillings to come inside the magic compound,
striking camp like Custer, recolonising the native ground.
On the beach we form a ritual circle, shake our heads in
disbelief at this fullness, making love less like a sin
than friendship, reaching out to touch the nameless other.
Pass each joint across, not to mere strangers but a brother.
Stoned, drowning in music that throbs sweet in scented air
so charged it can be touched. Beneath Afton Down we cast care
aside with clothes, to light our fragile way to illumination;
lost, weightless, we cascade down an avalanche of imagination.
Wild odysseys of guitars wind serpent-paths through the skies,
the glow of freedom coursing from our simple, blinded eyes.

As if it never happened! Under the wiles of post-modernism
our lives are jumbled out of context, a self-reflecting prism;
Aryan boys on *Top of the Pops*, brylcreemed brokers earning a packet –
'We're all Thatcherites now': our kaftan the waxed Barbour jacket.
Mass shooting parties stalk the streets of London, in leather and tweed.

Back here time atrophies. Fashion is landlocked. Content I go to seed
dreaming this Island, its ghostly heritage of mad, dissolute harmonies;
at the Bay the river Yar flows northwards to a distant, unimagined sea.

Outlaws hang together, out in the west; the longest village street
in England, Freshwater spreads itself like a giant's winding sheet.
As bungalows appreciate, the past is ransacked: immemorial acres
yield their names to housing developments, JCBs rip them like paper,
the spirit of landscape drips away. Here, the Who sang 'touch me,
feel me' across dark, incense-crazy fields, like a religion, freed
from history. Now it's back, the mating call of a new car.
This present is endless future, the worst of all worlds where we are.

I took, one winter's afternoon, a stroll across the golf-course,
past the tumuli and bunkers, a nuclear hide-out sunk deep in gorse,
the reservoir – hidden water, shrouded like a giant skull
by its carapace of turf – to the eighth tee, as the upturned hull
of Afton Down bends back to earth. There, in a green shade, I stumbled
down rabbit tracks and footholes, to squat on a molehill as if pulled
by sad memory to the valley below, that arctic prairie.
                                                    Where
half-a-million once sat, watching a makeshift stage – their
tents billowing beyond, a fairy-tale army – now the wind scuffed
mere grass, waving goodbye to all that passing show. Enough
to have been there, perhaps. And then from out the undergrowth a fox,
dead rabbit in its jaws, feeding its young. Like some spinning paradox
we faced each other, baffled enemies, each rooted in paralysis
till it scuffled away to nowhere. That is sufficient, *simply to exist.*

v. *Animals*

They always come when least expected;
young badgers turning white-faced from my car,
bitch fox lifting her disdainful stare.
They always come when most neglected.

I only see them properly in death;
a shrew, broken-backed and velvet,
bright cold eyes of a taken rabbit.
I only see them clear in death.

They hide in terror and in night;
not birds that flaunt their otherness,
not liquorice slugs revelling in excess.
They hide their sameness in the night.

vi. *Gone to Earth*

The heart's clockwork grows rusty as a used car, prey to infirmity;
retreat is the habit of these days, locking tight each fortress –
youthful fierceness yields to our desire, merely, to be.
I live on the fault-line, high on a cliff-top; my rural fastness
slopes off to the sea. Unsung, the landlord tills a vertical garden,
wrested from neglect, a maze of drunken tracks, tottering. They harden
into serpent paths, winding through a paradise of builders' rubble,
the waste land reclaimed. Snowdrops surface, like a corpse's stubble.

We too sow a wild harvest, stubborn weeds which choke the body politic,
kept alive on daydreams and 'cheap Bulgarian wine'. I am truly sick
of all the compromise, the shabby lies, the triumphs of mediocrity,
for nothing can still the vision of that celestial, dream city
we glimpse if deep in drink, or at the peak of love: "Fiddlers' Green".
Alchemists pitched both the everyday and paradise at this place, *Thalia*,
the head and tail of the cosmic snake, and what here most demeans
can also seed fruition, in genitals and guts. Our absurd Saturnalia.

I'm a cultural commissar; I serve on a cat's cradle of committees;
chair of one, tea-boy on another. Tribes reconvene for the winter
– darts' clubs and tea-dances, philately, devil-worship, yoga – these
drab, secret meetings in darkened rooms. Our local community splinters
like a smashed windscreen, gummed back together by the *IOW County
     Press*,
that suppository of gossip, as arcane as Urdu, or witchcraft, or chess.
Giants pace its *Letters'* column, calling up the muskets of civil war:
this Island breeds border feuds, each boundary dispute a running sore.

In the middle of life's maze, events reverse. I'm ever more aware of
mortality, go to more funerals than weddings, feel there a truer love
as wreaths of wild bluebells commemorate each new-dug grave. Earth
settles over, like an ancient barrow, like a goddess quick in birth –
what new age waits, thus nurtured? What future shivers in the night,
as unimagined as those who stalked the *sixties'* party, ripe for blood?
Fossils, we're pressured into living stone, crushed blind by appetite.
Who will resurrect us, retrieve fools' paradise from the enriching mud?

Adam's curse is upon me each morning. Strip lights flicker into life
and up the path they come, the lonely, curt and communal; they're all
on file, ticketed and ordered as a row of graves. Hidden like a knife,
each book holds secret indentations; hieroglyphs, circles, mating-calls.
They circle on this open place. Denizens of the spruce new bungalows,
the shabby out-of-season let, the manor house, the retirement close,
all make their mark: my congregation, to entertain and instruct. I loan
out dreams. Like spies, my library is dispersed into every home.

I pace the bars, the beaches, the barbecues, searching out lost volumes,
and lose myself in sunlight, buried alive on a crazy Sunday afternoon.
Anonymous, too, this Island. Its landscapes are worldly, infinite;
Bembridge is Hollywood, *St Saviour's*, *Totland* a campanile in red brick.
We light two candles, transfigured by the flame of what we truly are,
stirred by an unseen breeze. They stutter to extinction, like our lives
which fuse through mortality – the cooling furnace of this dying star –
into immanence. Flowers of fire, closed pathways to an empty sky.

vii. *Library Mystery*

The sudden, sick surprise of broken glass
as if a bird, trapped, had broken out
like some dreadful warning, or a shout
from the unseen adversary of a savage past.

But insight comes like dawn, merely a break-in.
Sullen daylight arrives with embittered cops,
the jovial *CID*. I phone my boss to own up
as if in complicity. Work yields to original sin.

And all is cleared up, except the crime – late
readers enter the unpadlocked library
once fingerprints are dusted, conformity
settles again to Agatha Christie on the rates.

Leaving dried blood on the windowpane, a calling card:

'*SORRY. TIMES IS HARD – A BURGELAR*'.

viii. *New Earth, New Heaven*

I'm late to bed tonight, she's already drunkenly asleep –
a recipe for trouble I could live on forever. Here we reap
wild oats into a settled harvest, in unholy domesticity,
like marble figures on a memorial tomb. Outside, the hungry sea
draws breath, but in this drey we're safely hunkered down;
red tufts of her fine-spun hair are spread across the eiderdown,
fairy gold. Jointly named on Xmas cards, my selfishness resigns

The great storm threw steps to the beach asunder. Realigned
like a child's crooked house, now they follow new contours
alongside which a scoop of cliff came down with wrecking force.
It glistens dully, blue slipper clay dripping down the cliffside
like run-down clockwork, trees horizontal in misdirected pride,
rooted in solid air. Everyday this cancer spreads, a wormy flood,
a tide of earth lapping the sea, slow-motion, a Passchendaele of mud.
This seething void settles to new, unimaginable acres,
seeding already with grass. Brutal process presupposes no maker,
rather how force can penetrate weakness, then rest insecure
until the next storm, or drought, or holocaust. Casualties of war . . .

ix. *Rough Trade*

I didn't realize he was going to hit her, honest. We'd
gone around to see this New-Age dealer, an entrepreneur
of 'antiques' which signified junk, and 'Mac the Stripper'
on the side – pine not prostitutes, but it provides the key.

It was about this train-set, rattling like a good yarn
around my childhood, going nowhere but magnificently,
tin-plate and clockwork, polished hard as teak, friendly
and dusted in its box, but broken. The spring was gone.

Anyway, along comes Mac, to deliver a rusty harmonium
stripped from some church: himself an instrument – of cash –
this man who knows the price and not the value, which clash
into the rough music of this age, its vain encomium.

So, he spots the artefact, it lights his touch-paper.
'Is this yours?' – yes – 'Can I take a look at it?' –
well, er, it does need repair, but I . . . and quick as shit
he's out the door like a weasel, slick as a Hollywood caper.

A month or two slips by, no word. Mac's gone to ground,
so we sniff him out. A rat we seek, not a full-blown fox,
slightly guilty till we track down his nesting-box,
a Georgian mansion on a private drive, a moated mound.

Up a steep slope we go, peasants rising above their station
– the train is gone – and indeed it has. 'It's been sold,
here's a fiver.' Mute incredulity makes us bold
enough to argue, derailing his guile with interrogation.

A mistake, of course; beaten in one sphere he can switch
tracks. 'Piss off,' he shouts: our feet take root
in disbelief. Suddenly she crumples like a parachute,
winded by his fist, then magically as if bewitched

she's flying out through the door, Charlie Chaplin
in a north-east gale, to crumple on the bottom step,
lifeless, a burst paper-bag, while Mac's kept
women sneers 'Incredible!' like a clockwork mannequin.

The door slams, just like the lid on a toy-train set,
boxing in brightness and innocence and betrayal
from the scalding air of enterprise. The timid fail,
the strong – literally – prosper. But I won't forget.

I didn't realize . . .

x. *Sandy*

What eyes still track lost stragglers from the feast of '69?
And who now sings the travellers, those driven out of line?
Your voice unwinds their visions and their flight,
those wayside outcasts, cowering in the night:
their sorrows join the sea.

What caused this barren ice-age, to freeze for twenty years
as – refugees – we hide behind the snowdrift of our fears?
And in your blood the snowflakes course and cling
yet, coiled and ever-flowing as a spring,
your song pours out to sea.

She died in April's thaw. The flood pulled her under its spate.
See it glisten from hill to hill, surge through fence and gate,
like some old ballad – dazzling, brutal, just.
Yielding a fresh-watered earth of human trust,
our sorrows join the sea.

xi. *Back of the Wight*

Across the Island's spine it runs, the old pre-Celtic trackway,
curving with the chalk from Culver to the Needles, Portland Bay
if the sea had not cut across, like the swathing embrace of time,
a rim of that ancient bowl of Wessex, our Goddess's lost shrine.
And here I stand, to measure our short-lived tenancy,
lost in a fold of green hills, at one breath from eternity.
It's the same sense of muted wonder as at remote Stonehenge,
a temple pointing, roofless, at the sky, or Avebury where bend
stones like broken teeth, enclosed – again – by that same circle,
the serpent always passing through. I feel that same full
quietude. The past laps quietly at our shores, eroding.
The past attempts desperately to reach us, encoding.

But here too are our ruins. Lost, stately Appuldurcombe,
opened by fire to burn away flesh to a skeleton of stone,
a temple to human folly. Why do we erect against our death
these baubles? At Ventnor, once, a child, I caught my breath
– my first memory – at the Island's diamond in a paddling pool;
it was worth my father's struggle down those cave-like hills. Fool
I came back an adult, once more to strut its largesse,
found instead a shrivelled, squalid shape, a tangled mess
of crisp packets, fag ends, dirt, drained for the season.
Yet still I jumped to crown my castle, lost to reason.

Yes, despite nightmare, we crowd to find a resolution;
carrion, we aspire to the divine. Near Chale's new confusion
I tracked past forbidden signs to reach 'Forgotten' Manor
its landlord proud to show a yew tree grown through the wall,
a well useful for three centuries, a tithe barn full of orchids.
In each suburban enclosure, a lost Eden lies somewhere hid.
Even Shanklin village, spruced antique for the tourists
– cream teas and thatched meals – can suddenly twist
the emotions like an errant puppy. Pink walls of Brading
conceal, past waxworked frissons, real bones decaying.

And maybe it's age or resignation, but some Sunday school
memory tugged a crisis back to prayer in a church's cool.
On a coastline of smugglers, where false lights beckoned
only to the sanctuary of rocks, tombs could conceal a reckoned
treasure, safe as death. Here too candlelight on stone
could promise a mystery, a way for solitude not to be alone.

Stone, not like at Bath a monument to Georgian splendour
or Oxford's cold precision, the intellect's surrender
to its own machinations, an arid sexlessness: –
here it survives, beaten, sensual, an acceptance –
that old pre-Celtic lodestone to set against the weather,
a metaphor for shared adversity, a talisman never
to die, setting our own skeletons against the wind.

At Mottistone, the old straight track leads to lichened
church up through bent oaks to the long barrow,
and at Godshill (aptly named) the options narrow.

Legend – the truer history – would have that church moved
from the valley, a coach-stop now choking on its fumes,
to the hilltop, 'Devil's Acre'. On that tumulus
it certainly rests secure. At the hidden terminus
of both ancient leys and Christian sacrifice, I look
at last on God's countryside, the man-stitched book
of fields and the eternal sea undermining, undermining.
I catch my breath at this timeless sense of hidden timing.

Inside, fading onto the wall on which so long ago painted,
gleams a lily cross, Christ in loneliness naked
and crucified, but smiling in his ever-human agony,
set against a wreath, a wedding gift, of pagan lilies.
The longstone and the cross are one, a culmination
pointing to eternity, to light our destination.

ON THE STRAND

Thalia

'The Sun is God', and here it is at last, resurrected
from indolent clouds, some child's lost beach-ball
falling slowly to a carrion sea. This alone we share,
that golden path to nowhere, but what we have neglected
wrecks the party – crowding a seafront cafe, we face the wall.
On Solent shore, cliffs horseshoe the echoing air.

At Totland, young Turner stole this shoreline's booty,
sketched fishing boats, decaying huts, the shifting land
and fixed it all on scrubby paper, fading into light.
I too am struck dumb with all its needless beauty,
blinded by waves, as an inky sea dissolves botched sand:
sunbeams fan the old pier's rotten underside like termites.

It's lost, that simple confluence of self and nature, pride
at our mastery ebbs like the waves, for here we slaughter
our birthright; its gold is tarnished, blood gluts our drains.
What I can't accept is that all is chaos, a dusty seaside
game whose sweet, peculiar variations we merely alter
to suit our own convenience, living each life in vain.

The play of sign and significance; we deconstruct this
wholeness to a void of mirrors reflecting nothing, scoff
where we should bend in prayer. No Muses sing our infinity.
Hurst floats unseen, lovely on the water, another Venice –
its lighthouse some doge's folly. Fishermen cast off,
pedalos weigh anchor, a silent tanker parades to an empty sea.

Maybe this is *Fiddlers' Green* and we're washed up, drowned
in Paradise, a lost and savage eternity we need
but can't believe. (If we smash the phone, it will never ring!)
Shipwrecked sailors enter such cold dreaming, unbound
until dragged back to life, choking in seaweed,
beached, gasping for white light where the angels sing.

No, it's real enough, this coastline. Here we seed
filth and broken bottles, but what we fail to take on board
leaves us stranded. Truth and beauty are connected
– on this Island, Keats faced a simpler, unpolluted sea –
but still we drown in emptiness, and cry for something more.
The sun is God, and here it is, at last resurrected.

Hard Cell

A man yearns from the juke-box, manufactured soul
which hits my own, sitting here on Poole quayside
in a tricked-out pub whose tricks are out of control;
portholes, ships in bottles, flotsam of the tide.

Was it last summer we sat here, mainlining Dorset ale
which does not dull but sharpens the fevered brain?
Your face bobs into my mind like a buoy in the tail
of a slipstream, an advert seducing me in vain.

The memorials of desire are sunken reefs, shoals
which catch us unawares, plunge us into feeling
when deep in work, rest or play – a rigmarole
we can't escape however we try; like chords unreeling.

The Ring of Kerry

I

TRIOLET

Her moods are like the seasons, implacable;
the sea beats on granite, reducing all to sand.
Between mountains coiled as beasts the tide is full,
her moods are like the seasons, implacable.
Dyed in blood, the harvest moon is merely beautiful
here where blind Amergin landed on the strand.
Her moon struck heart. Like the seasons implacable,
the sea beats on. Granite reducing all to sand.

II
AMERGIN'S SONG

I am the breeze which infects the sea,
I am the ravening tide, time's wrack.
I am the false witness of eternity,
I am the horned beast of sevenfold combat.

I am the vulture which scavenges these rocks,
I am the sickness of unconquered sunlight.
I am wild fuchsia by the shaken lough,
I am the sickle boar in rancorous delight.

I am the salmon leaping cold prescience,
I am the lake in which no fish dare swim.
I am the forbidden ballyhoo of science,
I am the cutting edge, your lust to win.

I am the godhead, who lit your eyes.
Who met you on the mountain? (If not I).
Who aged the yellow moon? (If not I).
Who eclipsed the dying sun? (If not I).

III
CONSEQUENCES

'It's the word of the truth,'
your uncle squeezing down pints, tiny
in his jovial paw, but then his number plate's 497 LIE;
as we stagger back that morning, sweet smoke edges an untroubled sky.

'That would be shamrock in our bog,'
clinging on for dear life, which explains
everything, our luck, turf laid like dark and bitter grain
outside the family ranch, drying in the wet, in the endless, sodding rain.

'Would you be having some holy water?'
Hopelessly Anglican, hypnotised by your aunt,
I nod assent, dreading some covenant, for her to grant
instead clear liquid dipped in double cream, fit for a god's restaurant.

'Pocheen is the work . . . of the Divil,'
thus some monstrous priest refusing to bury
two workmen dead of five bottles each, with which merry
truth we fall about like drunken skittles, joined by the whole Ring of
    Kerry.

An Italian Visit

This country is still in thrall to love-lorn Dante,
writing in exile his metaphors of heaven and hell
here made flesh, torn bleeding from the inanimate.
Through his lost city, vespas strut their pale riders,
ringing the Basilica in rounds of loud steel. Yet,
viewed from Fiesole, Florence is indeed Paradise.

I stand everywhere; in admiration at ruined Torcello –
the Virgin holding out her empty hands, lizards tilting
gravity sideways where Hemingway elevated the host
of male excess – in bars simply to save money.
High in a Medici palace, we make love beneath chandeliers,
and hell is simply your absence; I'm suddenly abroad.

Elsewhere, in the ugly outhouse of a public park,
you opened my eyes to Giotto's vast creation.
Christ's stare hypnotises Judas, toy buildings
frame a simple truth – tears which at first
resemble laughter. Art is not here a commodity
but a revelation, worthlessly frescoed on the wall.

.   .   .

53

We land finally in Venice, its horrible magnificence;
beauty mirrored exactly in the rotting canals.
East meets West in dying splendour, Guggenheim
buried with her dogs in a garden close to Eden –
marble statues front inpenetrable water, a guide intones:
'For state occasions, this horse has a detachable prick.'

Within earshot of the stazione, we erect nightly our
mysteries of flesh as vision; this decaying charnel-house
propels its own weird energy. Tintoretto's Christ rises
in San Rocco an astronaut crucified, catapulted underwater.
On the waterfront, a Yankee warship looms like darkness
above toy houses; black as history, moored on an inland sea.

Sitting near St Mark's, we watch the drunken sailors until
one approaches, a child safe from Libya's hell, shakes our
hands. 'It sure is a messed-up world we're living in.' Maybe
here, among treasures looted from Byzantium, purgatory might
unloose its meaning – this trashy earth undermined by water,
our bodies transcendent, the world resolved in fitful peace.

The Voyage Back

She only left memorials
sheets disarranged like a dream,
flowers hardening in a jar,
a thank-you note cold as the dawn –
she only left memorials.

The voyage back was ceremonial
that ship stately as a lost queen,
a cigarette and a beer at the bar,
my car waiting locked and forlorn –
The voyage back was ceremonial.

The difficulties of saying farewell –
a country where once I was king,
the dying gleam of an evening star,
bleak sunlight on the opposing shore –
The difficulties of saying farewell.

Festival

'Roll up, roll up for the first *Sealink Isle of Wight Festival of the Arts*. A great time is guaranteed for all.'

Festival Brochure.

It starts, of course, with a party. The Welfare State
are camped behind some nunnery, fruit-punch by candlelight,
our circle ritually fired. This decadent, unexpected Island
hazes into legend – a maze of fields, the asylum, the sea –
as all stumble to a taut rhythm; waves, madmen and ghosts
infused by this passing show, 'Engineers of the Imagination'.

In a cold age, money-changers market our imagination –
a commodity of profit and loss in the temple, a well-fed state
in which patronage patronises. Bright desire, though, ghosts
self-interest, banking on 'real gold', and moonlight
dawns like capital brought forward. Stony broke, lost at sea,
we still can dream – slow drowning – of treasure island.

A yuppie's dream home; Tennyson colonised his island
here, a treasure-house turned temple of his imagination.
Here we act Alfred, Watts, Mrs Cameron. The blank sea
of faces smiles – applause enriches Farringford's estate –
as, costumed and bearded in his den, we make light
of this our heritage, acting out the watching ghosts.

Another day, another deutschmark. I entertain ghosts –
Prince Albert's choir – scrubbed and compliant. The Island
pours, dissolved in rain. Undeterred, we soon alight
at Godshill for knick-knacks and the church. Imagination
kindled by Burts beer, we tour Brading waxworks as one states
'War is over' near a Gatling gun, near the pocked, gunmetal sea.

Exiles gather in the haunt of Apollo, poets whom this very sea
exhumed – Hooker, Hyland, Sean Street are disembodied ghosts
no longer. Each takes this poop-deck of a stage to state
how South turns in their guts like a fish-hook, childhood's island,
nostalgia hardened into art. One brings an axe lest imagination
fail me; 'I'll cut your head off otherwise.' I blind the light.

Back where King Charles was less fortunate, fire beacons light
Carisbrooke. Strange tales unreel of Tennyson wrecked at sea,
Mexicans pursued by a cactus. Thus, the communal imagination
yields a fiesta, a punk band hymning Victoria. The ghosts
are playful now, as darkness unravels, our sombre Island
flames into being, a barn dance with bagpipes. *Well fares this state.*

Mysterious, a darkness bounded by daylight
                    as her royal spirits dance for Osborne's ghost –
each footstep is a wave of the boundless sea,
                    of this timeless, haunted, joyful Island;
gone west the exuberant terror of imagination,
                    the dead join the living, in festival, in state.

Anchor

Hidden by the sludge of *everyday*,
you root me into mother earth,
an umbilical cord that prompts rebirth –
calm beneath the pointless surge of waves.

From stormy ocean, you always promise
a true resort; like the moon above
you silently draw me, with love
and with need. The safe harbour of your kiss.

Just Desserts

In this place, less a garden than a space among trees,
a summer house revolves like a fairground game. Timber
is planed to permanence, in whose circular fastness we
eat the fruits of summer, quaff strawberry wine, limber

up from conversation into communion, strangers into friends.
Half-light glimmers from the wood, a bat careers
crazily like our discourse, which through strange angles bends
into meaning. Enclosed yet open, the mundane disappears

into magic. Post prandial, we meander down Shanklin Chine
whose dizzying depths entrance, its steeps fruited with light.
Giant artichokes seem relics of this healing scoop of time;
one could imagine dinosaurs, here resurrected in the twilight.

And at the base, refreshment. We soak up beer and gossip,
watch the iridescence of waves which break forever on
this festive shore, then climb back where Keats once sipped
life like opium, through holiday chaos to a walled Elysium.

You talk of graveyards and the human spirit, beaten down
but everywhere resurgent, the absolute need to create
such epiphanies, such silence – the element in which we drown
finally to become parents, ancestors, the dead. This weight

of history draws me homeward, past lowering hedgerows and
the steady sea to my own silence, writing these very words.
Each generation, we make our imprint on the fresh-laid sand
for darkness, like a tide, to cover up, to render us unheard.

Three-in-One

HERITAGE

The wet romanticism of an English holiday,
as Uppingham glooms. Lost, we sip free coffee
in an over-priced bookshop, wishing it was tea,
and buy a memorial volume; G. K. Chesterton at play.

His paradoxes undermine this soggy dog's day.
Next door, Daedalus and sad minotaurs, a cold sea
of reflecting bronze; we view Ayrton's mazes for free
and traverse a bare landscape to lonely Fotheringhay.

Volvos circle the naked hilltop – stripped of stone –
where Crouchback was born, proud Mary beheaded,
but the pub serves 'baked apple with loin of pork'
as a stink of pig defines the clinging loam.
And we follow some broken thread, fail to inherit
our own country – chrome, gunmetal, each satisfied fork.

BEHEADED

Pork as a stink of pig.

Free lost Minotaurs and free sad Mary.

Gunmetal Volvos traverse a sea of bronze . . . next hilltop broken.

An English gloom threads Uppingham to Fotheringhay, defines this apple country, clinging and wet.

We follow a dog, view a door, book a tea-shop holiday. We fail and buy some volume coffee, soggy as day. G. K. Chesterton, baked at the pub, was the serve and play of a fork.

But of wishing, own.

DAEDALUS

Stripped, we inherit each loin's memorial,
for Ayrton's mazes circle naked stone.

Our heritage is bare, a lonely Romanticism;
crouchback, overpriced the reflecting loam.

I sip cold landscape, satisfied with paradox,
proud to undermine where I was born;

Home.

Cilla Black at Sandown Pavilion

ACT ONE

Outside, sand drifts like snow, black water waits slow crunching
on the old pier like lost applause. Inside we sit here munching
boiled sweets as sweet tension of hope deferred comes to the boil.
Lights ebb into darkness, robbing us of self-regard, of daily toil
to start the ceremony. A crackerjack host fizzles, gay as fireworks;
a medicine-man curing, with tablets of laughter, each sexual quirk.
Jovial as an unreal uncle, he threads each act with sugar, this
white-suited seagull, dumping laughter on our heads like . . . bliss.

Knowing bandsmen, jugglers toying with near disaster, a queer
trio of Latin gauchos, holding down guitars like naughty steers.
Mindless as TV, we clap obedience, foregather in the warmth
of darkness to swallow each course like gourmets; my paunch
aches now for respite – and relief! Just in time, we're
beached in light, blinky-eyed, marooned back on the pier.

ACT TWO

But it starts again, regular as by roughage the suited band
swirls out an overture like foreplay, both casual and planned,
Their twinkling brass and leery organ drum us to submission;
inert, laid back, waiting – we assume the *missionary* position,

And sudden as lightning, predated by our thunder, she comes
our goddess, carefully lit like a bus parading down Ryde prom.
Everybody's redcoat, red-haired and devious, from the chatty
plunging – just like that sea beneath – into the suddenly catty,
goosing her audience, hooting loud. The smoking bandstand
smirks too, masonic laughter; her pianist takes things in hand.

A bouquet of notes, shiny shoes on the pedals, his instrument
leads us out from harbour.
      Foghorn, then siren, she circumvents
time to young emotion, the cordite smell of black and white TV.
Her voice cuts into memory, 'our Cill' emoting here so free
like a songbird, a prostitute, a goddess; soft hands psalming
two decades of disappointment back to the playground, to cavern
down into a cellarful of noise
      Priscilla White, yet to earn
her rainbow, checking hats and talent, from slums of Scotland Road
released there to instinct, massive lungs set on overload.
The potent lure of cheap music, lullabying Liverpool, intent
on turning Lennon's imaginings from a possible world into lament.
Encores like matrimonial photographs, the same repeated ecstasies,
and away she wafts, like perfume, to sign cut-price LPs.

                . . .

ENCORE

Outside again, barred forever from this walled pavilion
we shuffle, her ghost still in each eye, dyed like vermilion.
The bar is catalogued with monochrome photos, all '*with love*',
a girl or maybe boy serves our desires; we both sip enough
to set us, sated, past bathing huts, past the loud choir
of angels to follow stars westward, to recollect desire.

All Saints

An angel folds its wings, huddled warm.
I pass by, cosy as the couples lying ended;
different dates, their joint lives ended
by a stonemason's chisel, 'greatly mourned'.

The boneyard ebbs down to the sea:
despite the yews, buds foretell the Spring.
Flowers die in jars, from death snowdrops spring,
gulls circle back like white débris.

I cloak in my warmth, feel its passing, but
walk towards the cold shore's culmination,
The church clock ticks towards culmination.
The lych gate swings sharply shut.

Ghosts

FUNERAL TEA

Once the heart's clockwork had stopped, you lay
so much dead weight, boxed and ready for burning.
In the middle of the aisle, a beached whale spurning
the funeral address like sawdust, your speechless braille

we read all too well, fumbling for our hymn sheets.
Six dying men shouldered arms. Centre stage
at last, how many words absorbed from all those plays
pecked round your bones, vengeful as gulls for meat.

The rest is silence, and we rested too at the abattoir,
a few mouthed words and off to the oven's heat
as outside twined flamed flowers of your wreath.
Communing on rolls that bridged sweetness to sour,
noisily we expunged your silence, cold meat
to tear at coffined in pastry, bloodied with tea.

II

LANE'S INN; RUINS

Where once families basked like sharks in sunlight,
hippies caroused by the moon, now timbers crack
with age, bricks expand to débris. The lack
of order unhinges mind and gateposts, mired with spite.

The sea still breathes heartlessly, drives an old couple
tottering past this ruin, seeing their own. A bulldozer
leans like a ship into destruction. Like a grocer's
piled display, the new flats mirror simply rubble.

Across a levered road, the next estate sits smug
hoarding roped-in grass, like its mortgages,
spruced clean as an Easter suit, squeaky with newness.
Yet the sea again portends ruin, the fug
of future years ghosts these mortices
and our bones, tears at our bright plumage.

III

OLD SOUTHAMPTON

Down in dockland, Tudor frames distend their bellies.
Misdirected to the city wall, I look down where shore
once ebbed, at matchbox cars cruising as if for whores,
sharp with life, coursing past swimming pool and factories.

Back at the pub, in the 'Knights', I strain for meaning.
A folk club prays upstairs, a singer cups his ear
to history, hiccuping through interminable slaughter,
here where Henry sailed for Agincourt. His keening

at last buries you, your difficult silences,
your hard-won faith I mocked, then imitated;
lost at sea, your voyage into endless light.
Life teems senselessly with new violence,
mocking in its circuits all that would negate it –
when the heart's clockwork has stopped, we lie.

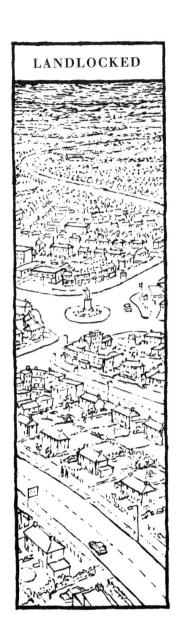

LANDLOCKED

Milton Keynes

'Till we have built Jerusalem . . .'

Sensible but lost, the new estates lie strangely dormant
in this dormitory town. Workers gain their nightly rest
as neatly as cars are parked beside each love nest;
newly settled. Walls crack, like a harbinger of torment.

Everywhere an absence. The force that planned these ramparts
bores the land into submission. Strict traffic lights
change pointlessly on empty streets, and delight
merely in symmetry, the blind insistence of the human heart.

No graveyards here, the tangled silences of history are
uprooted like dead elms, like people. New gods defend
these acres, for whom words become a colony, a snare.
We walk not Cemetery Road but *Larkin* Boulevard
– now safely dead – from *Chaucer* Close to *Tennyson* End;
will footsteps one day tramp my bones, in *Hinton* Square?